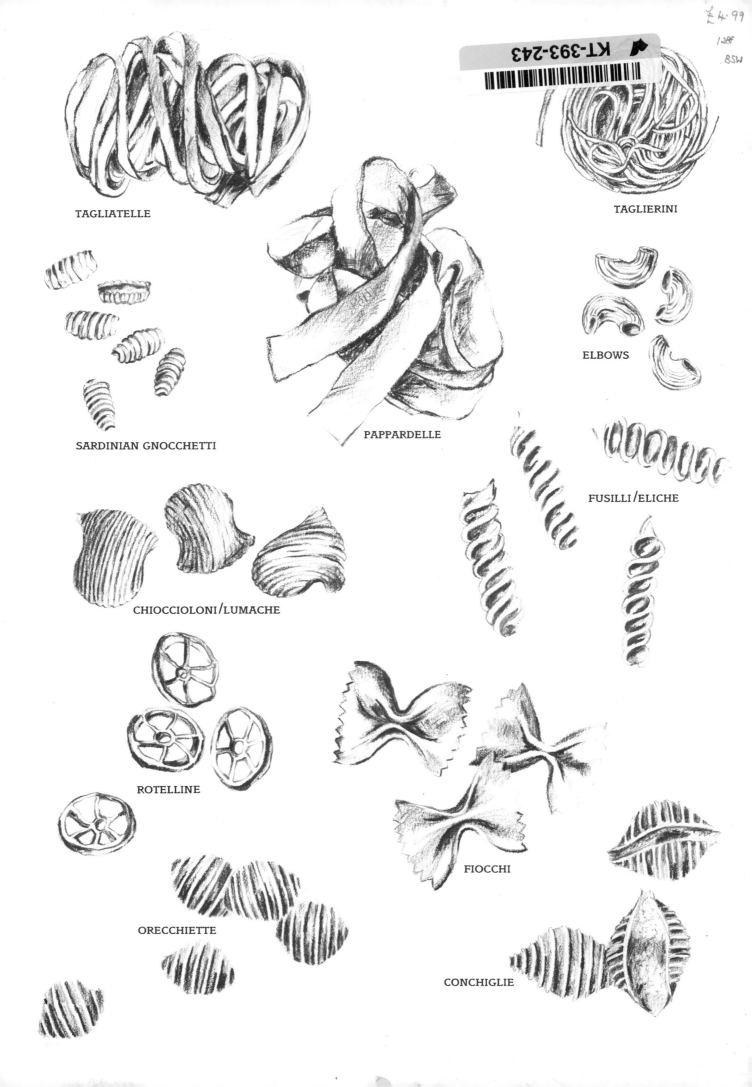

TAGLIATELLE

TAGLIERINI

SARDINIAN GNOCCHETTI

PAPPARDELLE

ELBOWS

CHIOCCIOLONI/LUMACHE

FUSILLI/ELICHE

ROTELLINE

FIOCCHI

ORECCHIETTE

CONCHIGLIE

EXOTIC PASTA

EXOTIC PASTA

70 new recipes for very different pasta dishes

Contessa Rossella de Angioy

Illustrations by Angela Chidgey

AURUM PRESS

Published by Aurum Press Ltd, 33 Museum Street, London WC1A 1LD

ISBN 0 906053 84 6

Designed by Neil H. Clitheroe
Colour separations by Culver Graphics Litho Ltd, High Wycombe
Typeset by Comproom Ltd, London
Printed in Italy by Sagdos

CONTENTS

Introduction

When writing about oneself one has to strike a delicate balance; it is all too easy to sound self-satisfied, and almost as easy to go to the other extreme and be too self-deprecating. I shall try to avoid both pitfalls and content myself with giving you a brief thumbnail sketch.

Although I was born in Florence, the first ten years of my life were spent in a little village by the sea, in Puglia, with my paternal grandmother. All my memories of those years with her are happy ones and it was, perhaps, during that time that my love of cooking and desire to know more about it were first awakened. In common with most of her contemporaries, my grandmother spent most of her time at home and found great fulfilment in seeing to every detail of the efficient management of her household, the most important realm being the kitchen. Although the cooking was simple, it was extremely varied and imaginative.

Then I went to live in Florence: life in a big city seemed like a different world to me after all those years in the country. It was a totally different way of living, with new tastes and experiences.

When still quite young I embarked on my career as a fashion model. During those years, when my work took me all over the world, I kept up my interest in cooking, which was heightened by the many different types of food I was able to try.

My second marriage, to a man who loved good food and knew a great deal about it, finally prompted me to start trying out some of the vast range of dishes which I had watched other cooks create for my delectation. My efforts were successful, if the favourable judgements of my guests are to be believed, and it was their encouragement which persuaded me to write this book.

Most of the recipes are quick and easy to prepare; I have aimed at collecting together a good selection of dishes which not only make the most of seasonal produce, but are also appropriate for different occasions and types of entertaining – catering for the varying tastes of family and friends.

Nowadays, most of us are simply not prepared to spend hours in the kitchen cooking each meal. For the most part our meals have been conditioned by the quickened pace of life: three light meals, the two main ones consisting of a starter, followed by a fish or meat dish and rounded off with ice-cream; or maybe a pasta dish and then a selection of cheeses and salads with fresh fruit to follow. This arrangement seems far more popular and practical than those long, leisurely lunches or dinners that I remember as a child when people consumed an incredible amount of food.

I remember the dinner parties I gave many years ago as a young married woman: a choice of two or three pasta dishes would be followed by an entrée and then a main course with a selection of vegetables. Several desserts were served, such as fruit flans and ice-creams or sorbets. Everyone used to tuck in with great gusto and all the food vanished amid talk and laughter. If I were to provide my guests with such variety and quantity today there would be lots of leftovers – many years too late for my sons to reap the benefit. When I entertained I always used to do all the cooking myself, sometimes for as many as fifty guests, and each time I calculated (wrongly) that there would be plenty left over for the two boys to enjoy; there never was.

Anyway, whatever your lifestyle, I hope you will derive as much pleasure from reading and trying out these recipes (and, of course, from savouring the results) as I have.

Buon appetito...

On cooking pasta

Remember that if you really want to cook authentic Italian meals you must follow that country's tradition of using very good raw materials; for instance, if a recipe calls for Parmesan cheese, make sure you buy the genuine article, in the piece, and grate some yourself as and when you need it. The same applies to other ingredients – the best olive oil, good unadulterated wines (which are not necessarily any more expensive), fresh herbs and the best fresh or more reputable brands of dried pasta, together with Italian cured meats and classic cheeses – all these will ensure that your dish is not just a faint echo of the original recipe.

We Italians find that cooking pasta properly comes naturally; for us it's a daily – if not twice daily – task.

Any self-respecting Italian needs to tuck into a plate of spaghetti at least once a day. My son Niccolo (now fifteen years old) was only nine when he began to learn how to cook spaghetti to the correct degree of tenderness and 'bite', together with a variety of suitable sauces.

I would, however, be the first to admit that even in Italy, the home of pasta, one sometimes comes across people who can't seem to learn the trick, and who overcook it.

But now let's get down to the serious business of learning to cook our delectable pasta. The first requirement is a large, deep saucepan which will hold at least 4½ litres/quarts; this will be sufficient to cook up to 800g/1¾ lb pasta. Secondly, make sure you buy the best pasta available, made with durum wheat flour. Lastly, always use coarse salt.

Bring to the boil plenty of water and add coarse salt to taste (err on the side of undersalting, which may result in rather bland pasta, rather than risk oversalting). Once the water has reached a fast boil, add all the pasta at once and stir a few times with a long-handled fork or wooden spoon to prevent any of it from sticking to the bottom of the pan. When the pasta is added the water temperature may fall below boiling point; if this happens, cover the saucepan immediately: the sooner the water comes back to a brisk boil the better. Stir again. As a very general rule, spaghetti takes 7-10 minutes but unfortunately it is impossible to lay down exact cooking times, since these vary with each different type of pasta — and when one reflects on just how many varieties there are, the problem is obvious.

The best advice I can offer is to test the pasta after seven or eight minutes. If it is tender but still offers a little resistance as you bite on it, then it is done (*al dente*). To keep your pasta at this perfect consistency, pour a cupful of cold water into the saucepan to stop the water boiling, and drain immediately.

When you have strained off all the water, waste no time in stirring in the sauce of your choice.

Pasta with herbs and aromatic flavourings

Taglierini with truffles

Serves 4
400 g/14 oz taglierini
1 truffle – preferably fresh but tinned will do (scrub or peel if fresh)
250 ml/9 fl oz/1-1¼ cups thick/heavy cream
50 g/2 oz/¼ cup butter

Melt the butter in a small saucepan, add the cream and heat while stirring for a few seconds.

Slice the truffle very thinly (there is a special little implement to do this, like a tiny mandolin slicer, but a very sharp knife will do), and add most of these wafer-thin slices to the sauce.

Cook the taglierini and drain, but not too thoroughly, and pour the sauce over the pasta. Scatter more truffle slivers over the taglierini and serve at once.

There is little point in specifying an exact quantity or weight of truffles – obviously the more of these fabulous fungi the better as far as you, your guests and their palates are concerned!

To follow this delectable first course, a fairly simple main dish such as chicken breasts in white wine with sauté potatoes would provide a good foil.

Spaghetti with butter and ginger

Serves 4
400 g/14 oz spaghetti
Small piece fresh root ginger
100 g/3½ oz/scant ½ cup butter
Small piece chilli pepper or pinch chilli powder
A few sprigs parsley

Melt the butter in a wide frying pan. Use a very sharp small knife to peel off the thin brown skin from the ginger root and cut off 5-6 wafer-thin slices (use more ginger if wished but not too much, or the flavour will be overpoweringly hot and strong).

Add the ginger slivers and the crumbled (or powdered) chilli pepper to the butter in the pan and sauté over a moderate heat for 3-4 minutes, stirring and turning once or twice so that the ginger does not brown. Keep warm over a very low heat while boiling the spaghetti.

Drain the spaghetti thoroughly; turn up the heat under the frying pan containing the butter, ginger and chilli pepper, and as soon as the butter starts to sizzle, add the spaghetti, stirring and turning over the heat for 1 minute so that it is thoroughly coated and flavoured with the butter mixture.

Serve immediately while still piping hot, adding the parsley to give an extra touch of colour and freshness.

Tortiglioni in piquant butter dressing

Serves 4
400 g/14 oz tortiglioni
10 spring onions/scallions
10 thin slices peeled fresh root ginger
100 g/3½ oz/scant ½ cup butter
Pinch chilli powder

Chop the onions, including their green leaves, into large pieces and brown them in the butter with the chilli and ginger for 5-6 minutes.

Cook the tortiglioni in plenty of boiling salted water until tender; drain well, mix with the hot butter dressing and serve.

Taglierini with rosemary

Serves 4

400 g/14 oz taglierini
150 g/5 oz/scant ¾ cup butter
5 sprigs fresh rosemary or 1-2 teaspoons powdered dried rosemary
1 chicken stock cube (or any light bouillon cube)
50 ml/2 fl oz/¼ cup single/light cream
Freshly grated Parmesan cheese

Melt the butter in a saucepan and add the stock cube and the rosemary. Stir with a wooden spatula or spoon until the cube has dissolved, and continue cooking until the butter turns golden brown. Add the cream and stir again.

Pour the piping hot sauce on to the cooked well-drained noodles and sprinkle with a little Parmesan cheese. Hand round a bowl of grated Parmesan for people to help themselves to more if wished.

Linguine with basil and black pepper

Serves 4

400 g/14 oz linguine
150 g/5 oz/scant ¾ cup butter
4/6 tablespoons finely chopped fresh basil
1 teaspoon freshly ground black pepper
50 g/2 oz/½ cup freshly grated Parmesan cheese

Melt the butter with the black pepper for about a minute in a small saucepan. Pour this on to the cooked drained linguine and stir in the chopped basil and grated Parmesan cheese.

Linguine, butter and lavender

Serves 4
400 g/14 oz linguine
150 g/5 oz/scant ¾ cup butter
3-4 sprigs fresh lavender
Freshly ground black pepper

Melt the butter in a small saucepan with the sprigs of lavender. When the butter turns a light golden brown, remove the lavender sprigs and discard. Take care not to let the butter burn.

When the linguine are cooked, drain well and cover with the butter sauce. Season well with a little freshly ground black pepper.

Spaghetti with fresh herbs

Serves 4
400 g/14 oz spaghetti
A sprig each of the following fresh herbs: thyme, tarragon, rosemary and dill
100 g/3½ oz/scant ½ cup butter
5 tinned tomatoes (or large, ripe blanched and skinned tomatoes)
1 chicken stock cube

Dissolve the stock cube in the melted butter over a moderate heat. Add the herbs and sauté for 2 minutes. Chop the tomatoes roughly, add them to the butter and continue cooking over a slightly higher heat for another 5 minutes. Serve on very hot cooked drained spaghetti.

If you have a balcony or are lucky enough to have a garden, be sure to plant these herbs. They are delicious and so useful for a wide variety of sauces. To accompany this dish, how about fillet/tenderloin steaks with green peppercorns or mild mustard and red wine?

Pasta with cheese

Fiocchi, ricotta and basil

Serves 4
40 g/14 oz fiocchi
250 g/9 oz/scant 1½ cups ricotta
Small bunch fresh basil
1 teaspoon freshly ground black pepper
50 g/2 oz/¼ cup butter

Wash the basil, remove the stalks and put the leaves into a food processor together with the ricotta cheese. Blend thoroughly until the mixture is smooth and an attractive, fresh pale green.

Drain the cooked fiochhi, leaving a very little moisture in the pan, and stir in the butter. Add the blended ricotta and basil and mix well. Sprinkle the pepper over the dish. If the ricotta mixture is too thick, making the dish too sticky, add 2-3 tablespoons of milk or hot water.

Tortiglioni, ricotta and saffron

Serves 4
400 g/14 oz tortiglioni
250 g/9 oz/scant 1½ cups ricotta
2 sachets pure saffron powder
½ medium-sized mild onion

Place the ricotta, onion and saffron in a food processor and blend thoroughly. Cook the pasta in plenty of salted boiling water until tender; drain off nearly all the moisture. Mix quickly but thoroughly with the cheese and saffron mixture, and serve hot.

Eliche with Gorgonzola and port

Serves 4
400 g/14 oz eliche
100 g/3½ oz/scant ¾ cup crumbled Gorgonzola cheese
100 ml/4 fl oz/½ cup single/light cream
50 ml/2 fl oz/¼ cup port

Cook the pasta in plenty of boiling salted water, and while it is cooking melt the Gorgonzola in the top of a double boiler or in a heatproof bowl over hot, but not boiling, water. Add the cream and port.

When the pasta is almost done, cook the sauce for 2 minutes over a direct low heat, stirring and scraping the sides of the pan with a wooden spatula. As soon as the pasta is tender, drain well and mix with the sauce. Serve at once on very hot plates.

Spaghetti, ricotta and chocolate

Serves 4
400 g/14 oz spaghetti
200 g/7 oz/scant 1¼ cups ricotta
50 g/2 oz/2 squares bitter chocolate
10 crystallized candied violets for decoration
Freshly ground black pepper to taste

Grate the chocolate and add half of it to the ricotta, working well with a fork until it is thoroughly blended.

Cook the pasta in plenty of boiling salted water; drain quickly and not too thoroughly. Stir in the ricotta and chocolate mixture and mix well; transfer to a serving dish and sprinkle with the rest of the grated chocolate together with a little freshly ground black pepper. Decorate with the violets and serve cold or just warm.

This is a very quick and easy recipe because it requires no further cooking once the pasta is cooked, and is an excellent way of using leftovers.

Chioccioloni with four cheeses

Serves 4
400 g/14 oz chioccioloni
50 g/2 oz/¼ cup Gorgonzola
50 g/2 oz/½ cup mascarpone (fresh double cream cheese)
50 g/2 oz/generous ¼ cup grated Gruyère cheese
50 g/2 oz/½ cup freshly grated Parmesan cheese
A little milk or cream as required

Mix the mascarpone and crumbled Gorgonzola cheese with the grated Gruyère and Parmesan, blending well with a fork.

Melt the butter in the top of a double boiler or in a bowl over hot, but not boiling, water and add the four cheeses, mixing well with a wooden spatula until the sauce is completely amalgamated. If it is too thick, gradually add a few spoonfuls of milk or cream.

Drain the cooked pasta, but not too thoroughly, mix quickly with the sauce and serve piping hot or the melted cheeses will thicken as they cool. Season with freshly ground white pepper if wished.

This dish might well be followed by a mixed salad. Some of my favourite ingredients are:
radicchio rosso (like red chicory in appearance)
Belgian chicory/endive
avocado slices sprinkled with lemon juice
apple slices
30 g/1 oz/¼ cup pine nuts
thinly sliced carrot
fresh dill
fresh tarragon
mustard and cress/mustard seeds (sprouted)
olive oil, salt and wine vinegar dressing

quattro formaggi

Penne with Stilton

Serves 4
400 g/14 oz ribbed penne
100 g/3½ oz/scant ¾ cup crumbled Stilton cheese
90 ml/3 fl oz/scant ½ cup single/light cream
50 g/2 oz/¼ cup butter
½ teaspoon paprika

Melt the Stilton in a pan over hot, but not boiling, water. When it has melted completely add the cream and butter. Over direct heat bring the mixture to simmering point while stirring continuously; be very careful not to allow it to stick to the sides of the pan, scraping away any deposits with a wooden spatula.

Meanwhile, cook the pasta in plenty of boiling salted water, drain briefly and stir in the sauce. Finish with a light dusting of paprika and serve hot.

Penne, cream and Fontina

Serves 4
400 g/14 oz ribbed penne
100 g/3½ oz/scant cup Fontina cheese
90 ml/3 fl oz/scant ½ cup single/light cream
Freshly ground black pepper

Grate the Fontina cheese very coarsely and melt in the top of a double boiler or in a heatproof bowl over hot, but not boiling, water together with the cream, stirring at intervals.

Cook the penne in boiling salted water; drain quickly and not too thoroughly, and pour on the cream and Fontina sauce. Stir very quickly to coat the pasta and then sprinkle with plenty of freshly ground pepper.

Serve piping hot, as the rich and velvety Fontina sauce will start to thicken if allowed to cool.

Do make sure you buy genuine Italian Fontina cheese from the Val d'Aosta, not the inferior Scandinavian imitations!

Pasta with vegetables

Tagliatelle with button mushrooms

Serves 4

400 g/14 oz tagliatelle
300 g/10 oz/2½ cups very small fresh button cultivated mushrooms
  or tinned champignons de Paris
500 g/generous 1 lb/2 ⅓ cups tinned tomatoes, drained and coarsely
  chopped
2 cloves garlic
Small bunch parsley
50 ml/2 fl oz/¼ cup olive oil

Clean and trim the mushrooms and slice them thinly with a sharp knife.
Slice the garlic into wafer-thin slivers. Sauté the mushrooms and garlic
gently in the oil in a saucepan for about 10 minutes. Stir in the roughly
chopped tomatoes and continue cooking for another 10-12 minutes.

Cook the tagliatelle, drain well and mix with the sauce. Dust with finely
chopped parsley.

This is a handy recipe, quick and delicious, using cultivated mushrooms
which are always readily available. Although lacking the outstanding
flavour of some wild mushrooms, there are cultivated varieties which
have plenty of taste and lend themselves to use in a variety of sauces for
pasta or meat.

Sardinian gnocchetti with pumpkin

Serves 4

400 g/14 oz Sardinian gnocchetti
400 g/14 oz/generous 2½ cups peeled, seeded and diced pumpkin
2 cloves garlic, crushed or finely chopped
100 g/3½ oz/scant cup grated pecorino cheese
80 ml/3 fl oz/scant ½ cup olive oil

Dice the flesh of the pumpkin and fry in the oil with the garlic, stirring and turning now and then, for about 10-15 minutes or until tender but not at all mushy. When cooked, stir in the drained gnocchetti and add the grated pecorino cheese. Serve hot.

Veal *alla pizzaiola* makes a very appetizing second course to follow this dish.

Spaghetti, aubergine and mozzarella

Serves 4

400 g/14 oz spaghetti
Approx 300 g/¾ lb aubergines/eggplants
1 mozzarella cheese weighing about 100 g/¼ lb, diced
1 clove garlic, chopped
2 or 3 sprigs fresh basil, finely chopped
50 ml/2 fl oz/¼ cup olive oil

Wash and dry the aubergines and remove the remains of the stem, but do not peel. Dice and sauté gently in the olive oil with the chopped garlic clove. Add a little more oil if necessary. When cooked, add the finely chopped basil.

Boil the spaghetti in a large pan of salted water until tender but still with a little 'bite' left and drain well before mixing in the aubergine sauce followed by the mozzarella, cut into small dice.

Serve on very hot plates; the spaghetti and sauce should be so hot that the mozzarella cheese starts to melt as it reaches the table.

Penne with broccoli

Serves 4

400 g/14 oz penne
400 g/14 oz fresh broccoli (or 1 large packet frozen broccoli, thawed)
1 clove garlic, chopped
1 teaspoon freshly ground black pepper
50 g/2 oz/½ cup flaked Parmesan cheese (see below)
100 ml/3½ fl oz/½ cup olive oil

Cut the broccoli into small pieces and fry gently in the olive oil with the chopped garlic clove in a large frying pan for 10-15 minutes. (If you are using frozen broccoli it will take less time – cook until tender but still firm.)

Cook and drain the penne and add to the broccoli. Stir together over a low heat for a minute or two to blend the flavours. Sprinkle with the flaked Parmesan and black pepper and serve at once.

If you buy Parmesan cheese from an Italian grocer or knowledgeable cheese merchant, it will be broken away from the cheese in rough lumps with a special, very strong, small leaf-shaped knife. As the piece of cheese is levered away from the cheese form, it splits along the natural lines of separation, according to the grain. You can then flake off small pieces of cheese from your own Parmesan with the tip of a short blunt knife. When the cheese is served in this way, the texture and full flavour can be fully appreciated.

Taglierini with artichokes

Serves 4
400 g/14 oz taglierini
2 large globe artichokes
200 ml/8 fl oz/1 cup single/light cream
50 g/2 oz/¼ cup butter
Freshly grated Parmesan cheese

Clean the artichokes, discarding the tough outer leaves and chokes, and slice them. Fry gently in the butter in a covered pan with 1 or 2 tablespoonfuls of hot water, making sure that they do not catch and burn (add a little more moisture if necessary).

When cooked, add the cream and reheat for a minute or two. Mix with the cooked well-drained taglierini and serve with freshly grated Parmesan cheese.

In Italy it is easy to find large tender artichokes, but the British or American cook may have to settle for tinned or frozen artichoke hearts, warmed through with the butter and water. Whole baby artichokes bottled in oil are sometimes available in Italian grocery shops, and these are young and tender enough to slice right through, using all the artichoke (having first drained off most of the oil). If fresh artichokes are used, rub with lemon juice as soon as they are sliced as the cut surfaces will otherwise darken and discolour.

Rigatoni with vegetables

Serves 4

400 g/14 oz rigatoni
1 medium-sized or 2 small courgettes/zucchini
1 small aubergine/eggplant
1 green pepper
2 heads or large spears of broccoli
2 cloves garlic, crushed
Pinch chilli powder
Small bunch basil, finely chopped
60 g/2 oz/½ cup freshly grated Parmesan cheese
100 ml/3½ fl oz/scant ½ cup olive oil

Clean and trim the vegetables and cut them into bite-sized pieces. In a large frying pan sauté the finely chopped garlic, the chilli and the vegetables in the oil over a moderate heat for 15-20 minutes, until lightly browned.

Taking care to leave the rigatoni *al dente*, drain and add to the vegetables in the pan, stirring for about 2 minutes over a slightly lower heat.

Serve very hot with finely chopped basil and a bowl of grated Parmesan cheese.

Taglierini with sweet and sour onions

Serves 4

400 g/14 oz taglierini
2 large onions
1 tablespoon wine vinegar
150 g/5 oz/scant ¾ cup butter
100 ml/4 fl oz/½ cup single/light cream

Slice the onions into thin rings and sweat them gently in the butter in a tightly covered heavy-bottomed saucepan. When they are cooked, add the spoonful of wine vinegar and stir for a minute with a wooden spoon.

Turn into a food processor with the cream and blend until the ingredients are well mixed and smooth. Reheat for a minute before serving on very hot well-drained taglierini.

Spaghetti with courgettes

Serves 4
400 g/14 oz spaghetti
Approx 300 g/¾ lb courgettes/zucchini
1 clove garlic, chopped
Small bunch fresh basil
50 ml/2 fl oz/¼ cup olive oil
Freshly ground black pepper
50 g/2 oz/½ cup freshly grated Parmesan cheese

Slice the courgettes into fairly thick rounds and sauté gently in the olive oil with the chopped clove of garlic. When they are almost cooked (after approximately 20 minutes) add the finely chopped basil.

Mix the courgettes into the freshly cooked drained spaghetti and season with plenty of black pepper. Sprinkle with grated Parmesan cheese to taste.

Short pasta with cauliflower

Serves 4
400 g/14 oz short pasta, such as sedani, mezzi rigatoni, cannolicchli
300 g/approx ¾ lb cauliflower florets
1 medium-sized onion
50 ml/2 fl oz/¼ cup olive oil
1 chicken or light stock cube
30 g/1 oz/¼ cup freshly grated Parmesan cheese
2-3 large ripe, blanched and skinned tomatoes or tinned tomatoes

Slice the onion into thin rings and break the cauliflower into very small florets. Soften the onion and cauliflower in the olive oil with the tomatoes, sautéing over a gentle heat in a large frying pan for about 3 minutes.

Dissolve the stock cube in a cup of boiling water and add to the cauliflower. Simmer for about 20 minutes or until tender, and mix gently but thoroughly into the freshly cooked well-drained hot pasta. Finish with the grated Parmesan cheese.

Penne, peppers and cream

Serves 4

400 g/14 oz penne
500 g/1 lb green peppers
250 ml/9 fl oz/generous 1 cup single/light cream
2 cloves garlic, crushed or finely chopped
Freshly grated Parmesan cheese
30 ml/1 fl oz/3 tablespoons olive oil, or more as required

Wash and dry the green peppers, remove the stalk, seeds and pith and cut into thin strips; fry gently in the oil in a non-stick frying pan with the crushed or finely chopped cloves of garlic for about 15 minutes, stirring from time to time. The shredded peppers will cook faster and will not burn if you cover the pan. When tender, put the peppers into a food processor with the cream and blend well.

Reheat the sauce for a minute or two, stirring with a wooden spatula, before mixing into the cooked well-drained penne. Serve hot with grated Parmesan cheese.

Ribbed penne with aubergine sauce

Serves 4

400 g/14 oz ribbed penne
1 large aubergine/eggplant (or several, weighing up to 300 g/¾ lb in total)
250 ml/9 fl oz/generous cup single/light cream
50 ml/2 fl oz/approx ¼ cup olive oil
1 clove garlic, finely chopped
Small bunch fresh basil, very coarsely chopped

Dice the aubergine and sauté in a large frying pan in olive oil together with the garlic.

When the aubergine is cooked (approximately 20-25 minutes), draw aside from the heat and add the chopped basil, reserving a few sprigs for garnishing.

Blend in a food processor with the cream until smooth and velvety in texture. Reheat this sauce over a moderate heat and pour it over the cooked drained pasta. Garnish with a little more fresh basil.

Spaghetti with radicchio rosso

Serves 4
400 g/14 oz spaghetti
100 g/3½ oz/scant ½ cup butter
Approx 300 g/¾ lb radicchio rosso
1 medium-sized onion
Freshly grated Parmesan cheese
Freshly ground black pepper
Pinch salt

Radicchio rosso, also known as Treviso radish, is like dark red and white chicory in appearance.

Clean and cut the radicchio into thin slices and chop the onion finely or slice into very thin rings. Heat the butter in a frying pan; add the radicchio and onion, cover and sauté, stirring from time to time with a wooden spatula. Add a little salt. The radicchio is ready once it has wilted and softened.

Mix the contents of the pan with the cooked well-drained spaghetti and serve very hot. Hand round a bowl of grated Parmesan cheese separately and have a peppermill full of black peppercorns to hand, for each person to add just as much cheese and seasoning as he or she thinks fit.

Orecchiette with Batavian endive, sultanas, pine nuts and anchovies

Serves 4

400 g/14 oz orecchiette
500 g/generous 1lb Batavian endive/escarole
40 g/1½ oz/¼ cup sultanas/seedless white raisins, soaked in warm
　water for 10 minutes
60 g/2 oz/⅓ cup pine nuts
6 tinned/canned or bottled anchovy fillets in oil
1 clove garlic, bruised by crushing lightly, but still whole
Pinch chilli pepper or small piece dried hot red chilli pepper
80 ml/3 fl oz/⅓ cup olive oil

Batavian endive or escarole is often sold when rather large in Britain and the United States; try to buy it when small and tender. Failing this, blanch for a little longer or substitute curly endive (sometimes confusingly referred to as chicory) which looks like a large curly green mop, or even small crisp lettuces.

Wash and trim the Batavian endive, cutting away the hard remains of the stem. Blanch for 3 minutes in boiling salted water; drain well and chop coarsely.

Heat the oil in a large pan and sauté the bruised clove of garlic until it begins to brown, then remove and discard. Add the Batavian endive, the previously soaked sultanas (well drained), pine nuts and drained anchovy fillets. Sauté while stirring and turning for about 10 minutes. Add the drained orecchiette (cooked *al dente*) to the pan and mix well for a minute or two before turning off the heat and transferring to a heated dish. Serve immediately.

This fresh-tasting first course would be very suitable to serve before a main course of game or a delicious roast of tender young lamb.

Penne and peperonata

Serves 4

400 g/14 oz penne
4 sweet (bell) peppers, preferably red and yellow
1 onion
Approx 50 ml/2 fl oz/¼ cup olive oil
Generous pinch of salt
1 clove garlic, crushed
Approx 500 g/1 lb/2¼ cups tinned tomatoes

Wash and dry the peppers, remove the stalk, seeds and pith and chop coarsely. Cut the onion into thin slices and crush the garlic.

Sauté all these vegetables in a frying pan in the oil until they have softened a little, and then add the drained chopped tomatoes. Add salt to taste and continue cooking for another 10-12 minutes.

Serve hot on the freshly cooked well-drained penne.

Fusilli with marrow flowers and mozzarella cheese

Serves 4
400 g/14 oz fusilli
10 marrow flowers
1 mozzarella cheese weighing about 150 g/5 oz
2 cloves garlic, finely chopped or crushed
80 ml/3 fl oz/⅓ cup olive oil
Pinch chilli powder or small piece dried hot red chilli pepper

Clean and trim the marrow flowers, removing the pistils. Heat the oil, chilli and garlic in a frying pan, then add the marrow flowers, cooking them for about 10 minutes or until they begin to turn pale golden brown.

Meanwhile, cut the mozzarella into small dice. Drain the pasta as soon as it is tender but still firm, add the marrow flowers and scatter the diced mozzarella over the top.

In Britain and the United States, serving this dish will be the happy privilege of those with a vegetable garden — it is a great pity that the marrow plants are in flower for so short a time. In Sicily one occasionally sees basketfuls of these flowers for sale, either at their peak in full bloom or, more often, slightly wilted but still a wonderful sunshine yellow colour, attached to one end of tiny marrows.

Penne, tomatoes, basil and black olives

Serves 4
400 g/14 oz penne
500 g/1 lb/2¼-2⅓ cups tinned tomatoes
50 g/2 oz/¼ cup butter
20 black olives, stones removed
Small bunch basil, finely chopped
Pinch chilli powder

Melt the butter over a gentle heat with the chilli powder for 2 minutes, then add the drained chopped tomatoes. Cook over a moderate heat for 15 minutes. Two minutes before removing the sauce from the heat, add the black olives.

Pour the sauce on to the cooked well-drained penne and sprinkle on the finely chopped basil.

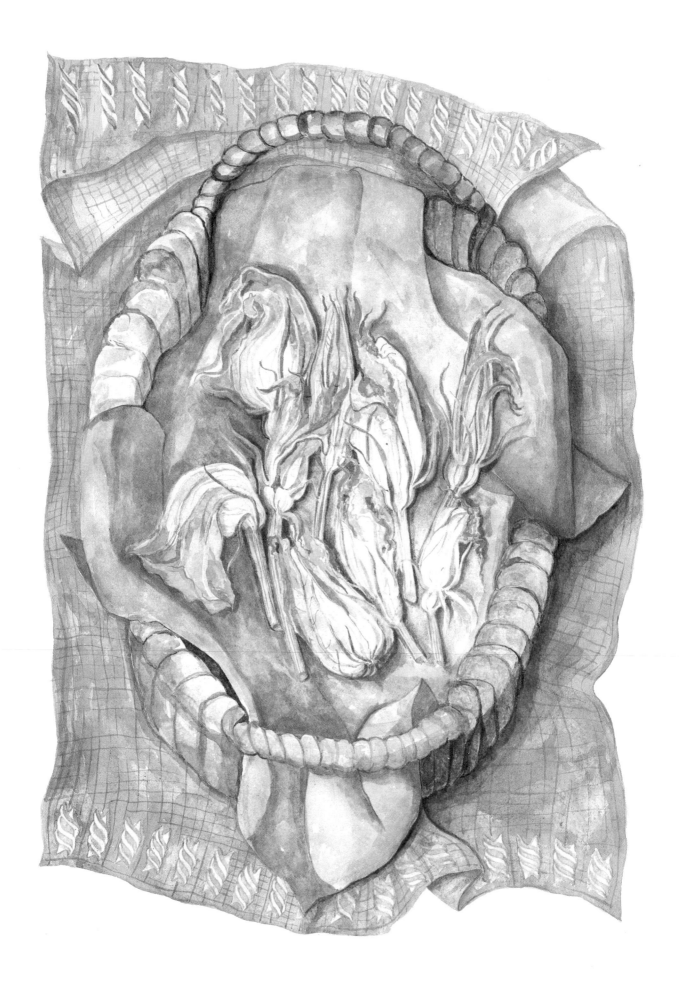

Forester's fusilli

Serves 4

400 g/14 oz fusilli

300 g/10-12 oz sliced *Boletus edulis* mushrooms (ask for porcini or cèpes if not readily known by this name) *or* 300 g/¾ lb/3 cups cultivated mushrooms

3 tablespoons finely chopped parsley (the flat-leaved variety if available)

1 large clove garlic, crushed or very finely chopped

Pinch chilli powder or small piece dried hot red pepper

50 ml/2 fl oz/¼ cup olive oil

If you cannot get *Boletus edulis* mushrooms (and do be careful if you are picking them yourself), this recipe is a delicious way of using cultivated mushrooms or any other variety of edible mushroom. Dried mushrooms can also be used: three of the 10 g/0.35 oz size packets, soaked in lukewarm water or a mixture of warm milk and water, will suffice for this recipe.

Clean the mushrooms carefully and slice them finely with a very sharp knife. Heat the oil in a frying pan with the pinch of chilli, add the sliced mushrooms and sauté gently for about 15 minutes with the crushed or chopped garlic and 2 tablespoons of finely chopped parsley.

When cooked, mix into the cooked well-drained fusilli and serve piping hot with a scattering of finely chopped parsley.

When wild mushrooms come into season at the beginning of autumn, one must seize the opportunity of being able to prepare all kinds of dishes in which they feature. For example, a menu based on wild mushrooms might include such dishes as: starters of wafer-thin slices of raw meat and imperial agaric (*Amanita caesaria*); forester's fusilli; pork fillets with *Boletus edulis* fried in egg and breadcrumbs and grilled *Boletus edulis* on a bed of toasted polenta slices.

Some varieties of wild or field mushrooms are delicious, some are merely unpleasant, while others can cause illness or even death. So great care is needed if you are gathering them yourself. Reputable greengrocers or specialist shops will take all the hazardous guesswork out of selection although the mushrooms will be expensive. The best varieties are the edible boletus or *Boletus edulis* (porcini or cèpes);

chanterelle (*Cantharellus cibarius*) and the morel (*Morchella esculenta*); while *Boletus scaber*, *Boletus badlus*, Imperial agaric and *Armillaria mellea* are pleasant tasting.

A good alternative is to buy dried mushrooms imported from Poland, Italy or Japan which are sold on strings or in packets (the former are better). These are soaked to soften and plump them up and may then be used in the same way as fresh mushrooms.

Sautéed tortiglioni and fennel

Serves 4
400 g/14 oz tortiglioni
Approx 300 g/¾ lb bulb fennel
50 ml/2 fl oz/¼ cup olive oil
Pinch chilli powder or small piece dried hot red chilli pepper

Clean and trim the fennel; slice from top to bottom in quarters or eighths, depending on size, and then cut the pieces in half so that they are not too long. Blanch in a large saucepan of boiling water for 2 or 3 minutes and drain well.

Heat the oil with the chilli powder or crumbled chilli pepper in a large frying pan and brown the fennel in this, turning frequently while frying for about 5 minutes.

Cook the pasta, and while it is still firm drain well and add to the fennel in the pan, stirring and turning while sautéing for 2 minutes. If you like your pasta more liberally dressed with oil, add 1-2 tablespoons when sautéing.

Make sure that the pasta is only just tender – drain it the moment it is *al dente*. This is important for this type of dish, when the pasta is to be cooked a little longer with the other ingredients.

Baked pasta dishes

Ribbed penne, mushroom and ham pie

Serves 4

400 g/14 oz ribbed penne
300 g/¾ lb/scant 3 cups very small button cultivated or tinned champignons de Paris
1 mozzarella weighing approx 100 g/¼ lb
200 g/7 oz/scant cup diced ham
50 ml/2 fl oz/¼ cup olive oil
1 clove garlic, chopped or crushed
Small bunch parsley, finely chopped

Clean and trim the mushrooms and cut into thin slices. Put the oil, garlic, chopped parsley and mushrooms into a saucepan and cook over a moderate heat, stirring and turning occasionally, for 10-12 minutes. Cut the cheese and ham into small dice.

Cook the pasta until *al dente*, drain well and stir in the mushrooms, ham and mozzarella. Transfer to a buttered ovenproof dish and place in a preheated hot oven (250°C/500°F/Gas Mark 9) until the cheese begins to melt and the pasta has browned a little.

All the oven-baked pasta dishes are very convenient and suitable when entertaining. Here are some more.

Layered penne, aubergine and tomato pie

Serves 4

400 g/14 oz ribbed penne
400 g/14 oz aubergines/eggplants
200 g/7 oz/1¾ cups mozzarella cheese
1 kg/2¼ lb/5 cups tinned tomatoes, coarsely chopped
1 clove garlic, crushed
Small bunch basil, finely chopped
30 ml/1 fl oz/3 tablespoons olive oil, sunflower or safflower oil
  for frying
Freshly ground black pepper

Trim, wash and dry the aubergines and cut into small dice. Fry in plenty of oil (use a deep-fryer if you have one) until they are a beautiful golden brown. Drain well on kitchen paper. Slice the mozzarella cheese.

Prepare the tomato sauce. Sauté the crushed garlic gently in the olive oil for 1 minute and add the chopped tomatoes. Simmer for 15-18 minutes and then add the finely chopped basil.

Cook the pasta so that it is tender but still very firm, drain well and add it to the aubergine with the tomato sauce, stirring well. Season with salt and freshly ground pepper to taste.

Pour half the mixture into an ovenproof dish, cover with a layer of the sliced mozzarella, and add the rest of the pasta mixture. Finish with a layer of mozzarella. Bake in a moderate oven (preheated to about 160-180°C/325-350°F/Gas Mark 3-4) for about 10 minutes, or until the cheese has melted.

Baked penne with Taleggio cheese

Serves 4

400 g/14 oz ribbed penne
300 g/11 oz/2½ cups Taleggio (or any of the Italian type of soft,
  buttery quick-ripening cheeses)
150 g/5 oz/scant ¾ cup butter
100 g/3½ oz/scant cup freshly grated Parmesan cheese
Freshly ground black pepper

Use ribbed penne for this recipe as they keep their texture and shape when cooked in this way.

Cook the pasta, being careful to drain when still very firm. Add three-quarters of the butter, ready melted with a generous seasoning of freshly ground black pepper, and mix well so the penne are well coated.

Cut the Taleggio into very thin slices.

Grease a deep oven-proof dish with the remaining butter and pour in half the pasta. Cover it with half the Taleggio slices and half the grated Parmesan. Cover with another layer of pasta and then top with final layers of Taleggio and grated Parmesan. Put the dish into a very hot oven, preheated to 250°C/500°F/Gas Mark 9, and bake until the cheese has melted and is beginning to brown (this will only take a few minutes). Serve at once.

Baked rigatoni with chicken giblets

Serves 4
400 g/14 oz rigatoni
400 g/14 oz chicken giblets
1 carrot
1 stick celery
1 small onion
1 thick slice bacon or salted pork (or pancetta) weighing about
    50 g/2 oz
1 kg/2¼ lb/5 cups chopped tinned tomatoes
50 g/2 oz/¼ cup butter (and enough to grease the ovenproof dish)
50 g/2 oz/1 cup fine fresh or dried breadcrumbs (not coloured or
    toasted)

Chop the carrot, celery and onion finely together. Melt the butter in a saucepan, add the vegetables with the diced bacon and brown lightly.

Clean, trim, wash and chop the giblets into small pieces and add to the saucepan, allowing the mixture to sauté and colour over a moderate heat for 15 minutes while stirring and turning now and then. Add the chopped tomatoes and continue cooking for another 15-18 minutes.

Cook the pasta and drain it while it is still firm. Butter an ovenproof dish and scatter some of the breadcrumbs inside it.

Mix the pasta and sauce well together and turn into the dish, scattering the remaining breadcrumbs over the top. Put into a preheated hot oven (230°C/450°F/Gas Mark 8) for about 15 minutes and serve piping hot.

Seafood pasta

Spaghetti with lobster coral

Serves 4
400 g/14 oz spaghetti
200 g/7 oz/scant cup lobster coral (roe)
100 g/3½ oz/scant ½ cup butter
1 teaspoon freshly ground black pepper

Melt the butter with the black pepper in a small saucepan. Add the lobster coral and sauté gently for 2 minutes. Cook the spaghetti so that it is still firm to the bite and drain. Add the sauce and serve piping hot.

It is not always easy to find lobster coral in any quantity on its own. When you are buying lobsters remember to ask for female (or hen) lobsters, and if you are lucky you can make this appetizing spaghetti dish.

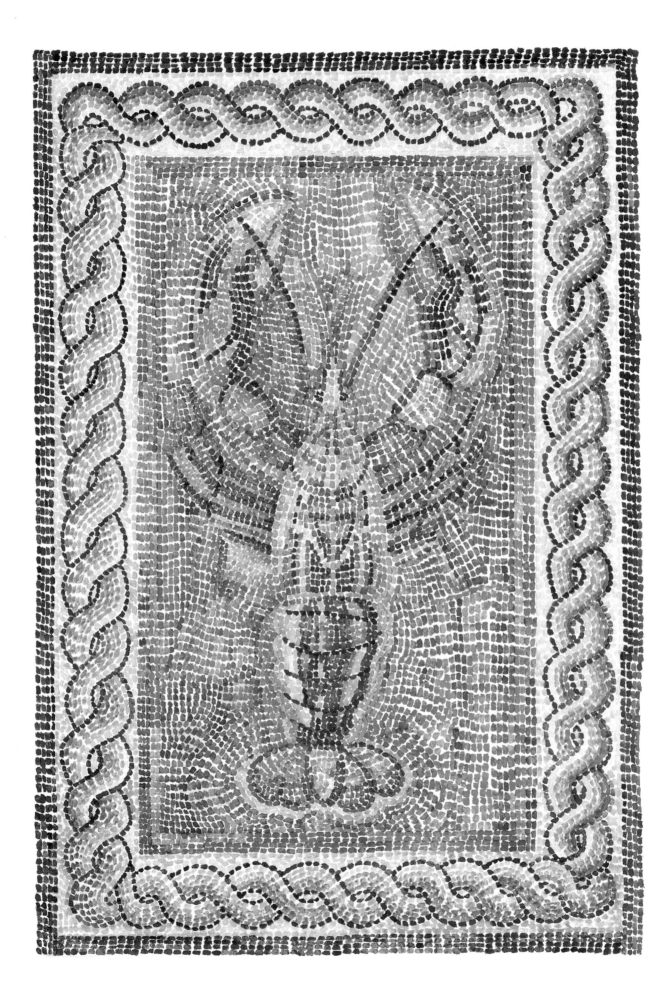

Spaghetti with lobster

Serves 4

400 g/14 oz spaghetti
1 small lobster, yielding 200 g/7 oz/1 cup flesh
80 g/3 oz/generous ⅓ cup butter
50 ml/2 fl oz/¼ cup brandy
Small bunch parsley, finely chopped

Boil the lobster for about 20 minutes, unless you have bought it ready cooked. Remove the flesh from the shell, (discard the gut and the stomach — located in the head) and cut into bite-sized pieces.

Brown the butter in a saucepan (*beurre noisette*), being careful not to let it burn, and add the lobster pieces, stirring for 1 minute. Add the brandy and simmer for 2 minutes, or until it has almost totally evaporated.

Drain the spaghetti, cooked but still *al dente*, and add the lobster and all its juices with a little finely chopped parsley.

A variation on this theme which is really delicious is a cold lobster dish. Toss the lobster pieces in a dressing of oil seasoned with finely chopped fresh parsley, garlic and salt and pepper. Cook the pasta until it is *al dente*, and then cool rapidly by leaving the strainer under cold running water. Drain well again. Add the seasoned lobster pieces in their dressing.

If a hen (female) lobster is used, include the coral in the dish — it will make it look extremely decorative.

Spaghetti, caviare and cream

Serves 4
400 g/14 oz spaghetti
150 g/5 fl oz/generous ½ cup single/light cream
150 g/5 oz/½-¾ cup caviare (or lumpfish roe)
1 teaspoon freshly ground black pepper

Scald the cream, turn the heat down as low as possible and add the caviare, warming it very gently indeed for 1 minute. Have the spaghetti ready cooked, still *al dente* and well-drained. Add the sauce and serve piping hot, sprinkled with black pepper.

Spaghetti with cod's roe

Serves 4
400 g/14 oz spaghetti
250 g/8 oz cod's roe unsmoked, fresh or tinned
50 g/2 oz/¼ cup butter
100 ml/3½ fl oz/scant ½ cup single/light cream
1 teaspoon freshly ground black pepper
Small bunch parsley, finely chopped

In a small saucepan melt the butter and heat the cod's roe, stirring well with a wooden spoon or fork to break up the roe. Add the cream while stirring continuously and cook for another minute.

Mix into the cooked drained spaghetti and serve piping hot with plenty of finely chopped parsley.

Seafood spaghetti

Serves 4

400 g/14 oz spaghetti
800 g/1¾ lb shellfish: clams, cockles or, ideally, Smooth Venus and mussels
Small bunch parsley, finely chopped
Small pinch chilli pepper or chilli powder
2 cloves garlic, crushed or finely chopped
100 ml/3½ fl oz/scant ½ cup olive oil

Clean the shellfish very thoroughly to remove impurities and sand, rinsing well. Place in a covered saucepan over strong heat until the shells open.

Remove from the heat and strain off the liquid that has collected, setting it aside after straining through a piece of cheese-cloth placed in a strainer.

Sauté the garlic very gently in the olive oil in a large frying pan and add the shellfish which have been half-prised or loosened from their shells. After a minute or two, when the flavours have blended, add the finely chopped parsley with the reserved shellfish liquor.

Add the cooked drained pasta and cook for another 2 minutes, stirring well. Take care not to overcook the pasta.

Serve piping hot with a little more finely chopped fresh parsley.

Spaghetti with buttàriga

Serves 4
400 g/14 oz spaghetti
80 g/3 oz/generous ⅓ cup smoked grey mullet roe
150 g/5 oz/generous ½ cup butter
1 teaspoon freshly ground black pepper
Small bunch parsley, finely chopped

Grey mullet roe, a Sardinian speciality, is sold in sausage shapes in some Italian delicatessens. Smoked cod's roe is a very good substitute — remove skin and any hard pieces.

Melt the butter with the black pepper. If Sardinian buttàriga is used, it is hard enough to grate; if cod's roe, rake over gently with the prongs of a fork to separate the eggs as much as possible.

Cook the spaghetti until it is *al dente* and drain well. Pour the melted butter over the spaghetti, mix quickly and then scatter in the roe and stir well. Garnish with the finely chopped parsley.

This is one of the quickest and finest sauces you can make. It has a superbly subtle flavour, and along with sliced fresh truffles it is one of the dishes I find most redolent of Italy.

If you care to continue with another fish course, try a firm-fleshed sea bream/porgy or imported Mediterranean dentex, poached whole, with avocado sauce.

Spaghetti with razor clams

Serves 4

400 g/14 oz spaghetti
500 g/generous 1 lb/generous 2 cups razor clams (fresh or tinned, imported)
500 g/1 lb/2 ⅓ cups tinned tomatoes, roughly chopped
50 ml/1½ fl oz/scant ¼ cup olive oil
Small bunch parsley
2 cloves garlic
Pinch chilli powder

Put the well-scrubbed razor clams in a covered heavy saucepan over a moderate heat for a few minutes. When they have all opened, remove from their shells and cut into pieces. Strain, reserving the liquor they have produced.

Meanwhile prepare the sauce. Heat the oil and chilli powder in a saucepan. Add the tinned tomatoes, roughly chopped, and cook for 10 minutes. Chop the parsley and garlic finely together and add to the tomatoes, together with the clams. Add about ⅓ cup of the reserved liquor. Allow the flavour to develop for a further 5-6 minutes while simmering gently. Serve hot on cooked drained spaghetti.

Razor clams – long tubular bivalves – are often hard to buy in most parts of Great Britain and the United States, although they are delicious raw or cooked and are plentiful in the inter-tidal areas of beaches in many parts of the world. In parts of Scotland, however, they are gathered in quantity and fully appreciated.

This is my sons' favourite dish and we thoroughly enjoy it whenever we go to the seaside, especially as razor clams are so cheap. Afterwards we always have grilled, freshly caught swordfish steaks. Delicious!

Spaghetti with scorfano

Serves 4

400 g/14 oz spaghetti
Scorpion fish weighing about 300-400 g/¾ lb
2 cloves garlic, finely chopped or crushed
Small bunch parsley, finely chopped
500 g/1 lb/2 ⅓ cups tinned tomatoes, chopped
50 ml/2 fl oz/¼ cup olive oil
Pinch chilli pepper

If scorpion fish (an extremely spiny fish) is unobtainable, substitute lobster flesh, monkfish or angler-fish.

Have the fishmonger gut the fish, or clean it very thoroughly yourself, removing the fins.

Prepare the sauce. Heat the oil and garlic for 1 or 2 minutes in a saucepan before adding the chopped tomatoes. Cook for 10 minutes.

Add the fish whole (or in the piece if part of a larger fish is used) and continue cooking for another 10 minutes or until the fish is done. Scorpion fish is ready when the eyes turn completely white and opaque.

Take up the fish from the sauce, bone it and return to the sauce to reheat. Cook and drain the pasta and cover with the fish in its sauce, garnishing with finely chopped fresh parsley.

This recipe is particularly delicious if you can manage to get the fish really fresh. Imagine lunching in the open air by the sea or enjoying supper with friends in the evening, out on a boat, with this dish as a first course followed by grilled freshly caught fish and mixed salad. With plenty of good dry white wine, naturally!

Linguine with inkfish

Serves 4

400 g/14 oz linguine
300 g/¾ lb inkfish/cuttlefish (choose the smaller, more tender
  specimens)
50 ml/2 fl oz/¼ cup olive oil
2 cloves garlic, finely chopped
Small bunch fresh parsley, chopped
Pinch chilli powder
125 ml/4 fl oz/½ cup dry white wine
50 ml/2 fl oz/¼ cup single/light cream

Clean the fish, removing the flat white 'bone', cutting away and discarding the eyes and hard parts and the yellowish deposit under the head; carefully remove and set aside the sacs containing the ink. Cut the tentacles and body of the fish into thin slices using a very sharp knife.

Heat the oil, the chilli powder and the garlic in a saucepan for 1 minute, then add the inkfish and most of the chopped parsley; cover and allow to cook gently for 20 minutes.

Pour in the white wine, turn up the heat and cook briskly for 3-4 minutes. Add the ink from the sacs and the cream and continue cooking for another 5 minutes.

Drain the linguine when they are *al dente* and add the sauce, stirring well. Garnish with the finely chopped parsley.

Be sure to try out this recipe when you next find fresh whole inkfish on sale at your fishmongers. However, tinned inkfish can be used so long as they are canned with their ink; they will need very little cooking. This is a special dish — the inky black linguine are very different from standard pasta. Don't let your guests in on the secret; let them enjoy guessing!

Spaghetti, beans and caviare

Serves 4
400 g/14 oz spaghetti
100 g/3½ oz/½ cup boiled white haricot/navy beans
100 g/3½oz/½ cup caviare (or lumpfish roe)
1 small mild onion or shallot
50 ml/2 fl oz/¼ cup olive oil

Chop the onion very finely and add to the beans and oil in a bowl. Allow the flavours to develop for a few minutes. Cook and drain the spaghetti in the usual way and add the chopped onion, beans and oil. Finally stir in the caviare gently.

This dish combines the subtle flavour of caviare – very expensive – with the more homely but tasty and nutritious beans.

Tagliatelle with tuna fish and tomatoes

Serves 4
400 g/14 oz tagliatelle
250 g/8 oz tin tuna fish
500 g/1 lb tinned tomatoes, drained and coarsely chopped
1 clove garlic, crushed or finely chopped
Small bunch parsley, finely chopped
50 ml/2 fl oz/¼ cup olive oil

To make the sauce, heat the oil and add the crushed or finely chopped garlic and the tomatoes. Cook for 10-12 minutes.

Add the tuna fish (drained if tinned in oil) with most of the finely chopped parsley and cook for 5 minutes more. Serve hot on cooked drained tagliatelle, garnished with a little more fresh parsley.

If you are in a hurry and want to eat pasta with a fish sauce, this is the quickest recipe I know, and very tasty indeed.

Linguine with crab

Serves 4
400 g/14 oz linguine
6-8 crab claws — raw or cooked
500 g/1 lb/2 ⅓ cups tinned tomatoes, chopped
Small bunch parsley, chopped
1 clove garlic, crushed or finely chopped
Small pinch chilli powder
Approx 100 ml/4 fl oz/½ cup olive oil

Remove the flesh from half the crab claws, leaving the others intact for decoration.

Prepare a very light tomato sauce. Heat sufficient olive oil to cover the bottom of pan and add the roughly chopped tomatoes with the finely chopped parsley, the crushed or chopped garlic and the chilli powder.

Bring to the boil and cook fast for 10 minutes with the lid off to allow the sauce to reduce and thicken a little. Reduce the heat and add the crab claws and the crab flesh. Cook for another 5-6 minutes so that the flavours are well blended. If raw crab claws are used cook for a little longer. Take up the whole claws and set aside.

Drain the cooked linguine and mix in the sauce, transfer to a heated serving platter or dish, garnishing with chopped parsley and placing the whole claws on top.

Obviously you can save time and trouble by buying about 200g/6-7 oz/1 cup of raw white crab meat rather than doing all the work yourself; in this case buy smaller claws for decoration.

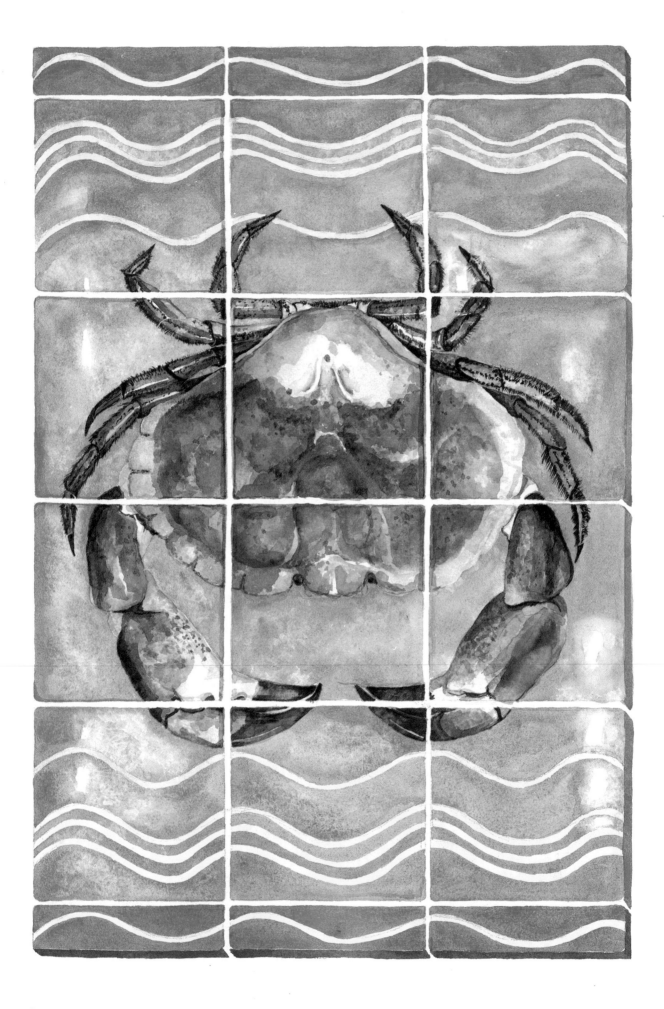

Pasta with fruit

Chioccioloni with peaches

Serves 4

400 g/14 oz chioccioloni
100 g/3½ oz/generous ½ cup bacon (or Italian pancetta – cured belly of pork)
100 g/3½ oz/scant ½ cup butter
2 fresh peaches, sliced
½ medium-sized onion or 1 shallot
50 ml/2 fl oz/¼ cup double/heavy cream
Freshly ground black pepper

Dice the bacon or pancetta and chop the onion; fry gently in the butter for 5-6 minutes. Add the sliced peaches and cook for 10-12 minutes. Stir with a wooden spatula from time to time; about 1 minute before serving, add the cream. Remove from the heat.

Drain the chioccioloni as soon as they are done and mix quickly with the piping hot sauce, seasoning with freshly ground black pepper.

Conchiglie with pork and pineapple

Serves 4

400 g/14 oz conchiglie
100 g/¼ lb/¾ cup fresh or drained tinned pineapple chunks
200 g/½ lb tenderloin/fillet of pork
1 small onion or shallot
50 ml/2 fl oz/¼ cup olive oil
Small pinch chilli powder
30 ml/1 fl oz/3 tablespoons red wine

Thinly slice the onion and sauté in the oil with the pineapple chunks and the chilli powder. When the onion is light golden brown, add the pork, very thinly sliced.

Cook until the meat is done (approx 30 minutes), adding the wine about half-way through the cooking time. Drain the cooked pasta and top with the sauce and pork.

I often use fruit in my cooking, either in this kind of recipe as a sauce, or as a side dish to accompany meat. I find the combination irresistible — imparting a fresh and unusual flavour.

Penne with orange butter and black olives

Serves 4

400 g/14 oz penne
150 g/5 oz/scant ¾ cup butter
Peel of a large orange
20 black olives, chopped

Using the nutmeg (very fine) side of a grater, grate the zest off a large orange, being careful to leave the white pith behind.

Melt the butter and orange in a small saucepan and heat for 1 minute. Add the chopped olives and cook for another minute. Pour over the cooked drained penne, mix quickly but thoroughly and serve piping hot.

The essential oils contained in the orange peel impart an incomparable flavour to this dish, mingling with the rich taste of the black olives.

Spaghetti and orange

Serves 4
400 g/14 oz spaghetti
1 large orange
150 g/5 oz/scant ¾ cup butter
Small pinch chilli powder
30 ml/1 fl oz/3 tablespoons Grand Marnier liqueur

Melt the butter with the chilli powder. Cut four horizontal slices from the orange (discarding the two end pieces); cut each slice into quarters. Sauté very gently for 5 minutes in the chilli butter, adding the Grand Marnier (or orange Curaçao or Cointreau) after 2 minutes. Cook very slowly so that the butter does not burn.

Cook the spaghetti until just tender and drain. Add the sauce and serve piping hot.

If you have run out of food but have an orange left in the fruit bowl, do try this sauce. It gives spaghetti a touch of novelty and solves the problem of producing an interesting lunch or dinner at short notice.

Penne with butter, strawberries and cream

Serves 4
400 g/14 oz penne
50 g/2 oz/¼ cup butter
Approx 250 g/9 fl oz/1¼ cups single/light cream
15 large strawberries plus a few small strawberries to garnish

Blend the large strawberries and cream in a food processor. Melt the butter in a saucepan and add the blended strawberries and cream; allow the flavours to develop over a low heat for 2-3 minutes.

Serve on cooked drained penne and garnish with a little ground black pepper and the small strawberries.

This recipe is excellent if you want to serve something new and intriguing to friends for lunch, especially if you have only a few minutes for preparation. Or perhaps you'd like to serve a meal with a pink theme: after pink pasta, try shrimps in a pink sauce (mayonnaise flavoured with a little tomato paste perhaps?) or a salmon mousse followed by a pink grapefruit sorbet.

64

Pasta with meat and game

Sardinian gnocchetti in chicken liver sauce

Serves 4

400 g/14 oz Sardinian gnocchetti
4 chicken livers
Sprig fresh sage, finely chopped, or ¼ teaspoon dried sage
50 ml/2 fl oz/¼ cup olive oil
Small onion, thinly sliced
Small pinch chilli pepper

Rinse and dry the livers, cut away any discoloured (yellowish or greenish) parts and gristle and chop them roughly.

Heat the olive oil gently in a frying pan over a very low heat – it should not be too hot. Add the finely chopped fresh or dried sage, the chilli and the thinly sliced onion. Sauté for a minute or two.

Add the chopped liver and cook very gently while stirring occasionally for 10-15 minutes. Don't cook the liver for too long or it will become tough.

Cook and drain the gnocchetti and mix in the chicken liver sauce. Serve piping hot.

Pappardelle with pheasant broth

Serves 4

400 g/14 oz pappardelle

Young hen pheasant, weighing about 500 g/1-1¼ lb, plucked, singed
and drawn

½ onion or 1 shallot, chopped

1 stick celery

1 clove garlic

1 sprig rosemary

Pinch red chilli pepper

Approx 225 ml/8 fl oz/1 cup red wine

250 g/9 oz/1¼ cups tinned chopped tomatoes

80 g/3 oz/6 tablespoons butter

40 g/1½ oz/scant ¼ cup fairly fat bacon, diced

Chop the celery, garlic and rosemary finely. Melt the butter in a pan, add
the celery, garlic, rosemary, chopped onion, diced bacon and chilli
powder and sauté gently for a few minutes until the onion and bacon are
lightly browned.

Cut the pheasant into small portions (leaving it on the bone at this
stage) using poultry shears, and place in the pan. Brown for a few
minutes and then add the wine; continue cooking for a few minutes more
until the wine has reduced considerably. Add the tomatoes and simmer
for about 1 hour, or until the pheasant meat will come away easily from
the bones.

Remove the pheasant pieces, take the flesh off the bone and return the
meat to the juices and liquid in the pan to heat through.

Cook and drain the pappardelle and cover with the pheasant sauce.

For this recipe you can use just the carcass of the pheasant (yielding
plenty of tender breast meat), keeping the legs for another recipe. An
older hen or cock could also be used since the dish is cooked slowly and
for long enough to tenderize all except the tougher birds, but the meat
does not have the moisture and flavour of the young hens.

The dish involves quite lengthy (but not complicated) preparation, but
if you have time to spend in the kitchen, do take the opportunity of trying
out this typically Tuscan dish – you will surprise your guests and perhaps
even yourself.

To go with this dish make a macedoine of vegetables (diced carrots,
turnips, chopped French/green beans, etc.) in a béchamel sauce, baked
in the oven.

Penne in stracotto broth

Serves 4

400 g/14 oz penne
600 g/1¼ lb beef joint (rump/top or bottom round)
30 ml/1 fl oz/3 tablespoons olive oil
1 carrot
1 stick celery
1 medium-sized onion
Small bunch parsley
Sprig rosemary
2 slices lemon
4 small pieces orange zest
1 kg/2¼ lb/generous 5 cups tinned tomatoes, chopped
225 ml/8 fl oz/1 cup dry red wine

Wash and dry the meat thoroughly, rub all over with salt and pepper and tie up securely.

Chop the carrot, celery, onion and herbs finely and put in a large, heavy-bottomed saucepan or cooking pot with the oil, lemon and orange zest. Sauté for 5 minutes.

Add the meat and brown for 10 minutes, turning the meat frequently and stirring well so that the herbs do not catch and burn. Add the wine and simmer, turning the meat once or twice, for about 10 minutes. Add the tomatoes (do not drain), and cook for a good hour with the lid on over a moderate heat until the sauce has reduced and thickened and the meat is done. Turn the meat once during cooking.

Remove the meat and set it aside to rest, as it will then be easier to cut into thin slices. Reserve some of the cooking liquid.

Drain the cooked penne while they still have a certain amount of 'bite' to them and stir into the remaining broth in the saucepan for a minute over a moderate heat. Serve the piping hot pasta and the carved slices of beef, moistened with the reserved liquid, in separate dishes.

Sometimes eating well involves a little more time. This dish can be prepared the day before, however, and all you need to do on the day itself is cook the penne and reheat the broth.

This is a marvellous dish for winter. When chestnuts are available try serving a dessert of sieved, slightly sweetened cooked chestnuts, topped with vanilla-flavoured sweetened whipped cream to follow (often known as Mont Blanc). If fresh chestnuts are not available, you can use dried ones (soaked until soft) or tinned chestnut purée. This makes a well-balanced menu which is sure to be extremely popular.

Penne with sausages

Serves 4

400 g/14 oz penne
200 g/½ lb pork sausages (preferably the small highly flavoured Italian variety)
70 g/2½ oz/5 tablespoons butter
½ teaspoon freshly ground black pepper

Skin the sausages and fry them in the butter for 10 minutes in a non-stick frying pan, turning and stirring. Cook and drain the penne and mix in the butter and sausages. Serve hot with freshly ground black pepper.

Sardinian gnocchetti with casseroled rabbit

Serves 4

400 g/14 oz Sardinian gnocchetti
400 g/¾-1 lb rabbit, jointed
½ onion, finely chopped
1 stalk celery, finely chopped
1 carrot, finely chopped
Small pinch dried rosemary, crumbled or powdered
Small pinch chilli pepper
50 g/2 oz/¼ cup fairly fat bacon or pancetta, diced
50 g/2 oz/¼ cup butter
250 g/9 oz/generous 1¼ cups tinned tomatoes, chopped
125 ml/4 fl oz/½ cup dry red wine

Wash the rabbit and cut it into 6 or 8 pieces; place in a non-stick saucepan over a moderate heat for 5-6 minutes, turning once or twice, to draw out the excess moisture.

Drain off and discard these juices and then add the butter, the finely chopped onion, celery and carrot, the rosemary and chilli pepper and the diced bacon to the rabbit in the pan; sauté while stirring and turning until everything is well coloured.

Add the wine and allow to simmer until it has partially evaporated. Add the tomatoes, cover the pan and cook over a gentle heat for about 1 hour, or until the rabbit is very tender.

When cooked remove the rabbit, bone it and return the meat to the pan to heat through. Pour over cooked drained gnocchetti.

This dish will take some time to prepare but is well worth the effort. You can try it out in winter, maybe while you are staying with friends in the country, when you want to savour something new (and very economical!). Serve with game paté spread on small pieces of toast which have been cut into triangles, diamonds, etc.

Pasta with spirits and spices

Tortiglioni with curry and walnuts

Serves 4

400 g/14 oz tortiglioni
80 g/3 oz/⅓ cup butter
2/3 tablespoons mild curry powder
1 medium-sized onion, finely chopped
1 stock cube
225 ml/8 fl oz/1 cup water
100 ml/3½ fl oz/scant ½ cup single/light cream
6 walnuts, shelled and chopped or 12 walnut halves, or 30 g/1 oz/
   ⅓ cup chopped walnuts

Prepare the curry sauce. Heat the butter with the curry powder, add the finely chopped onion and cook over a moderate heat for a few minutes. Crumble in the stock cube and add the water, stirring until dissolved. Cook over a moderately high heat for 10 minutes or so to reduce considerably before stirring in the cream. Drain the tortiglioni thoroughly when tender and mix with the sauce and the chopped walnuts.

Spaghetti with saffron

Serves 4

400 g/14 oz spaghetti
1 medium-sized onion
3 sachets powdered saffron
50 g/2 oz/¼ cup butter
250 g/9 fl oz/1¼-1½ cups single/light cream
50 g/2 oz/½ cup freshly grated Parmesan cheese
Freshly ground black pepper

Cut the onion into thin slices and fry gently in the butter in a saucepan. When the onion is a light golden brown add the saffron and the cream, stirring with a wooden spatula. Bring to the boil and simmer for 2 minutes, stirring from time to time.

Cook and drain the spaghetti and pour on the sauce, mixing thoroughly. Season with black pepper and sprinkle with Parmesan cheese to taste.

I love the flavour of curry, and in spite of the fact that it is not widely appreciated in Italy, I use it frequently to add an exotic flavour to some Italian dishes. It is a great standby when you have unexpected guests and there is next to nothing in the store cupboard because it keeps well and is always handy. If you are not a frequent user of curry powder, however, buy very small tins as the spices lose some of their flavour and aroma as time goes by. It is also good as a seasoning sprinkled very sparingly over salad.

Penne with vodka

Serves 4
400 g/14 oz penne
500 g/1 lb generous 2½ cups tinned tomatoes, chopped
1 medium-sized onion
50 ml/1½ fl oz/scant ¼ cup vodka
50 g/2 oz/¼ cup butter

Chop the onion very finely. Melt the butter in a saucepan, add the onion and sauté until soft and pale golden brown. Add the chopped tomatoes and cook for 15 minutes over a fairly high heat. Add the vodka and simmer for another 5-7 minutes.

Cook and drain the penne and serve piping hot, mixed with the sauce.

Vary the spirit used to your taste: whisky, Drambuie or brandy (cognac or armagnac) are variations on the theme of this recipe. If you have friends who like to drink, you can give them a lot of pleasure by making this dish using their favourite tipple.

Cold pasta dishes

Chioccioloni with chicken, onion and mango

Serves 4

400 g/14 oz chioccioloni
1 chicken breast weighing about 200 g/½ lb
1 small to medium-sized green mango (preferably Indian)
1 medium-sized mild/Bermuda onion or 4 spring onions/scallions
½-1 teaspoon mustard seed, according to taste
50 ml/2 fl oz/¼ cup olive oil or walnut oil
Freshly ground black pepper

Poach the chicken breast with some herbs or vegetables (celery, carrot, bay leaf, etc.) to add flavour. When cooked, remove the meat from the cooking liquid and cut it into small bite-sized pieces. Peel the mango, remove the stone and cut into thin slices. Slice the onion into very thin rings.

Make a dressing with the oil (use a little more if necessary to coat all the pasta), plenty of salt and pepper and the mustard seed, and mix it with the rest of the ingredients into the cooked, cooled and well-drained pasta. (The pasta may be cooled rapidly by being left in a strainer under cold running water).

Rotelline with yoghurt

Serves 4
400 g/14 oz rotelline
250 g/9 fl oz/1¼-1½ cups yoghurt
100 g/3½ oz/1 cup peeled, diced cucumber
1 small onion, roughly chopped
1 clove garlic
Freshly ground black pepper

Blend the yoghurt, cucumber, onion and garlic in a food processor. When smooth, season with salt and pepper.

Cook and drain the rotelline and refresh under cold running water. When cold, drain well and dry briefly in a clean cloth to ensure that the pasta will not make the sauce watery. Mix thoroughly with the sauce and serve.

Greek-style yoghurt is best for this recipe as it is very mild and creamy.

Spaghetti, tomatoes, basil and black olives

Serves 4
400 g/14 oz spaghetti (or almost any other type of pasta)
Small bunch fresh basil
3 or 4 large tomatoes (about 400 g/14 oz) blanched and skinned
100 g/3½ oz/²/₃ cup black olives
50 ml/2 fl oz/¼ cup olive oil
Freshly ground black pepper

Dice the tomatoes; remove the stones from the olives and the stalks from the basil. Toss in olive oil as if making a salad and season with salt and pepper. Set aside for up to 15 minutes.

Cook the pasta until it is *al dente*, drain it and cool rapidly by placing in a strainer under cold running water. Mix the well-drained pasta thoroughly with the dressing, using more oil if necessary to coat the pasta. Serve cold.

If you think you may want to add salt to this dish, have sea salt on the table rather than adding it to the dressing; salt will draw the moisture out of the tomatoes very quickly and make the dressing distinctly watery!

Penne, tuna, onion and French beans

Serves 4
400 g/14 oz penne
250 g/9 oz tin tuna
1 medium-sized mild/Bermuda onion
200 g/1 lb French/green beans
125 ml/2 fl oz/½ cup olive oil
Freshly ground black pepper

Trim and rinse the beans and cook them in simmering salted water for a few minutes. Do not overcook, they should still be firm and slightly crisp to the bite.

Cut the onion into very thin slices and add to the well-drained beans. Add the tuna, coarsely flaked with a fork. Dress with oil, salt and freshly ground pepper and add to the cooked, drained cold pasta.

Soldiers' pasta

Serves 4
400 g/14 oz ditali
2 or 3 large, firm, but ripe tomatoes (about 300 g/¾ lb)
Small bunch fresh basil
150 g/5 oz/generous cup very fresh mozzarella cheese
50 ml/2 fl oz/¾ cup olive oil
Freshly ground black pepper

Preferably use the classic buffalo milk mozzarella, obtainable from good Italian grocers.

Blanch and skin the tomatoes before dicing. Cut the mozzarella cheese into fairly small dice and chop the basil leaves. Mix these ingredients with the olive oil, salt (preferably sea salt) and plenty of freshly ground black pepper as this dressing must season the pasta well. Leave for 15 minutes or so to allow the flavours to develop.

When the pasta is cooked but still *al dente*, drain and refresh under cold running water. Drain very well and mix thoroughly with the dressing.

This dish owes its name to the fact that ditali was the type of pasta most frequently served up to Italian soldiers when they were in barracks.

Regional pasta dishes

Naples
Spaghetti with clams

Serves 4

400 g/14 oz spaghetti
1 kg/2¼ lb fresh carpet-shell clams (*Vongola verace, Vongola nera*), or 250 g/½ lb tinned clams, drained
500 g/1 lb/generous 2½ cups tinned tomatoes
1 clove garlic, finely chopped or crushed
Small bunch parsley, finely chopped
50 ml/2 fl oz/¼ cup olive oil

Clean the clams if they are fresh and still in their shells, discarding any which are damaged or open. Place them in a closed pan over a moderate heat until the shells open. Remove them from their shells.

Prepare the sauce. Sauté the garlic in the oil in a large pan for 1 minute. Add the tomatoes and cook for 15 minutes. When the sauce has reduced and thickened, add the clams and the chopped parsley and allow the flavour to develop for 3-4 minutes.

Cook the spaghetti so that it is still very firm to the bite, drain and add to the pan, mixing into the sauce. Serve with more finely chopped fresh parsley.

Puglia

Orecchiette with bread sauce

Serves 4

400 g/14 oz orecchiette
150 g/5 oz/1½ cups fine, soft brown breadcrumbs
500 g/1 lb/generous 2½ cups tinned tomatoes, chopped
50 ml/2 fl oz/¼ cup olive oil
1 clove garlic, finely chopped or crushed
Small pinch chilli pepper
2-3 large sprigs fresh basil
60 g/2¼ oz/generous ½ cup grated caciocavallo cheese (mature
   variety, a spun curd cheese like provolone)

Use brown bread which is at least 3-4 days old to make fine
breadcrumbs, using a food processor or grater, or simply cut the loaf in
half and rub the two cut surfaces against each other.

Sauté the garlic gently in the oil with the pinch of chilli pepper. Add the
breadcrumbs and fry gently while stirring, browning them for about 1
minute, being careful not to let them burn.

Add the chopped tomatoes and simmer for about 15 minutes: the
sauce should reduce and thicken a little.

Cook the orecchiette, drain and mix into the sauce. Transfer to a
heated serving dish, scatter the grated cheese on top and garnish with a
few fresh basil leaves.

I always love cooking orecchiette because they remind me of my
childhood. They are delicious all the year round and that touch of basil
highlights the flavour of the cheese.

Lazio

Penne all'arrabbiata

Serves 4

400 g/14 oz penne
500 g/1 lb/generous 2½ cups tinned tomatoes, chopped
3 cloves garlic, finely chopped or crushed
2-3 sprigs fresh parsley, finely chopped
Large sprig fresh basil, finely chopped
Generous pinch chilli powder
50 ml/2 fl oz/¼ cup olive oil

Fry the garlic and chilli in oil in a large frying pan until a good deep golden brown, but be careful not to let them burn. Add the chopped tomatoes and cook for 10 minutes. Stir in the finely chopped parsley and basil.

Cook the pasta so that it is still *very* firm to the bite and add it to the tomato sauce in the pan; continue cooking while stirring for a minute or so, to allow the pasta to absorb some of the flavour.

Serve hot with more chopped fresh basil if wished.

The exact quantity of chilli is a matter of personal preference — it depends how 'hot' you like it (literally, *arrabbiata* means angry). In any event, don't be too heavy on the chilli, or the flavour will become almost bitter and you will ruin the whole dish.

Lazio

Spaghetti alla carbonara

Serves 4

400 g/14 oz spaghetti
150 g/5 oz/¾ cup pancetta or fairly fat bacon
50 g/2 oz/¼ cup butter
3 large fresh eggs
50 g/3 oz/scant 1 cup freshly grated Parmesan cheese, or use half
**   Parmesan and half pecorino cheese (the latter has a stronger taste)**
Freshly ground black pepper

Try to find Italian pancetta as its distinctive flavour is necessary for this dish to taste really authentic.

Dice the pancetta or bacon and fry it in the butter until it has browned a little and begins to crisp and curl up. Break the eggs into a bowl and beat well before adding the grated cheese, or cheeses, blending thoroughly.

Cook the spaghetti so that it is just tender and still very firm. Drain briefly; add the egg mixture, stirring briskly off the heat to avoid curdling the egg. Quickly add the hot bacon and go on stirring. Serve hot with freshly ground black pepper.

Abruzzo

Bucatini alla matriciana

Serves 4

400 g/14 oz bucatini
200 g/½ lb/1 cup fairly fat bacon or pancetta, diced
1 onion
500 g/1 lb/generous 2½ cups tinned tomatoes, chopped
80 g/3 oz/¾ cup grated pecorino cheese
50 ml/2 fl oz/¼ cup olive oil
Large pinch chilli pepper

Chop the onion and add it to the oil and chilli in a saucepan. Sauté for 2 minutes, then add the diced bacon and continue cooking for 5-6 minutes. Add the peeled, chopped tomatoes and simmer, stirring occasionally, for 10-12 minutes (it should reduce and thicken slightly).

Cook and drain the pasta when still firm to the bite, add the sauce and top with the grated pecorino cheese.

Tuscany

Pasta and beans

Serves 4

300 g/10½ oz short pasta or ditalini
250 g/9 oz tin white haricot/navy beans
50 ml/2 fl oz/¼ cup olive oil
Sprig sage
Sprig rosemary
2 cloves garlic, finely chopped
Small pinch chilli pepper

This is the quickest way to make a tasty meal of beans and pasta.

Fry the garlic, sage, rosemary and chilli in the oil (reserve 1 tablespoon) until it takes on a little colour. Add the contents of the tin of beans, including the liquid, and cook for about 15 minutes.

Meanwhile cook the pasta, drain when it is still very firm to the bite, and add to the beans. Cook for a minute or two, until the flavours have mingled.

Serve hot, with a tablespoon of olive oil whirled on top.

This dish is also very enjoyable when just warm. Like the following recipe, it makes a good hearty winter meal. We need to eat food which is higher in calories to give instant energy when it is cold. I often serve rabbit or chicken *alla cacciatora* (Hunter's rabbit or chicken) with it. A good red wine, maybe a young Chianti, would set this menu off to perfection.

For this and the recipe opposite you can use up all the broken pieces of pasta of various shapes and sizes which inevitably accumulate.

Tuscany

Pasta with chick peas

Serves 4
300 g/10½ oz short pasta
250 g/9 oz chick peas/garbanzos
2 cloves garlic
Sprig rosemary
50 ml/2 fl oz/¼ cup olive oil
Small pinch chilli pepper

Follow the same method as for *Pasta and beans* (opposite page).

In these two recipes I have specified tinned beans and tinned chick peas, purely because the preparation and cooking time is so much shorter. I can assure you that the resulting dish is every bit as good, as long as you buy reputable brands of both products.

Tuscany

Spaghetti, butter and tomatoes

Serves 4

400 g/14 oz spaghetti
1 kg/2¼ lb ripe fresh tomatoes, halved
1 carrot
1 stick celery
2 cloves garlic, crushed
1 medium-sized onion
2-3 sprigs parsley
Large sprig basil
80 g/3 oz/⅓ cup butter
Freshly ground black pepper
100 g/4 oz/1 cup freshly grated Parmesan cheese

Place the halved tomatoes in a large pan with all the vegetables and herbs, season with salt and pepper and cook over a moderate heat with the lid on for about 30-40 minutes. When ready pass the sauce through a Mouli-légumes or sieve, so that the tomato seeds and vegetable fibres are left behind and can be discarded.

Cook the spaghetti until it is *al dente*, drain well and stir in the butter, followed by the sauce and Parmesan cheese. Serve piping hot, garnished with a few fresh basil leaves.

Make this sauce in the summer when tomatoes are at their peak and store in small quantities in the freezer. Then in the depths of winter you can bring back summer with the unique flavour of fresh tomato sauce. In my recipes I often use tinned tomatoes because they are so handy — in fact, I don't know what we would do without them. But the flavour of fresh tomato sauce is quite unbeatable.

Liguria
Trenette with basil sauce

Serves 4

400 g/14 oz trenette
1 large bunch fresh basil weighing about 100 g/3½ oz
80 g/3 oz/scant cup pine nuts
2 cloves garlic
150 g/5 fl oz/generous ½ cup olive oil
100 g/3½ oz/scant cup freshly grated Parmesan cheese
30 g/1 oz/2 tablespoons butter
1 medium-sized potato, unpeeled
100 g/¼ lb French/green beans
Freshly ground black pepper

Blend the olive oil, garlic, pine nuts, Parmesan cheese, the leaves of the basil minus the stalks and salt and pepper to taste in a food processor until you have a very smooth, thick sauce. (The traditional method of making this sauce, *pesto genovese,* calls for a large pestle and mortar to pound all the ingredients together, the oil being added a little at a time.) Place the potato (cut in half) in a saucepan of cold water with a little coarse sea salt; bring to the boil, add the beans and pasta. When cooked, drain lightly, reserving the water, and cut the potato into small pieces. Mix the sauce into the pasta and vegetables. Stir in the butter and the remaining Parmesan cheese.

If the mixture seems too thick, add a spoonful or two of the hot liquor in which the vegetables were cooked. Serve immediately.

This is a really delicious sauce, and the Genoese use it all the year round on such dishes as boiled vegetables, fillets of meat cooked *alla Milanese*. If the cheese is omitted and the amount of pine nuts increased, it sets off boiled or poached fish to perfection; a spoonful can be added to bouillon or hot consommé, or use it simply to add interest to a plain hard-boiled egg. It is easy to prepare the sauce when basil is plentiful and freeze it until needed. On the day, all you need do is thaw it and use it to enliven almost any dish you like, with a little butter and grated cheese.

Liguria
Linguine with walnut sauce

Serves 4
400 g/14 oz linguine
100 g/3½ oz/1 cup walnuts
1 clove garlic
100 g/3½ oz/½ cup butter
80 g/3 fl oz/generous ⅓ cup single/light cream
80 g/3 oz/¾ cup freshly grated Parmesan cheese
Freshly ground black pepper

Blend the walnuts, garlic, butter, cream, salt and pepper very thoroughly until you have a smooth sauce. Cook the pasta and drain it lightly, reserving a little of the water, and mix the pasta with the sauce. Add the grated Parmesan cheese, and if the sauce seems too thick add 1 or 2 tablespoons of the water reserved after boiling the pasta.

This is a *pesto* and, like the more familiar Genoese *pesto* made with basil and pine nuts pounded in a mortar, it can be made in advance and kept in the refrigerator or freezer until needed. It is advisable to use the very best quality walnuts or the sauce may have a faintly rancid or bitter after-taste.

Notes on the illustrations

Page 19   The lavender in this picture was picked in Tuscany and the bee represents the Barberini bee, the insignia of a famous Italian family.

23   This magnificent animal, which is still used for ploughing, lives on the farm next door to my house in Tuscany.

27   The background design is from a fabric in a fresco by Benozzo Gozzoli in the Medici Chapel, Florence, 1460.

31   This is based on an early Italian still-life painting.

35   The decorative border is taken from an Italian Maiolica plate in the Victorian and Albert Museum, London.

39   The flowers were bought on market day in Colle Val d'Elsa, Siena.

43   This has been adapted from a fourteenth-century marble pavement, the Wheel of Fortune, in Siena Cathedral.

47   This mosaic was influenced by many early Roman examples in collections in Rome, the British Museum and the Victoria and Albert Museum.

51   The twisted motif for the spaghetti was used extensively by the Romans in decorative work.

55   This eighteenth-century Italian plate is in the Victoria and Albert Museum.

59   The Italians are famous for manufacturing and using tiles.

63   This border design and colouring was taken from a fresco in the Etruscan Museum, Villa Giulia, Rome.

67   This design is from a seventeenth-century table-top made of scagliola.

71   The background is gnocchetti and the design on the rabbit casserole is taken from Italian Maiolica.

75   These illuminated letters were inspired by some found in the Piccolomini Library in Siena Cathedral and date from the fifteenth century.

79   This is after a fresco in Pompeii of the Birth of Venus.

Index

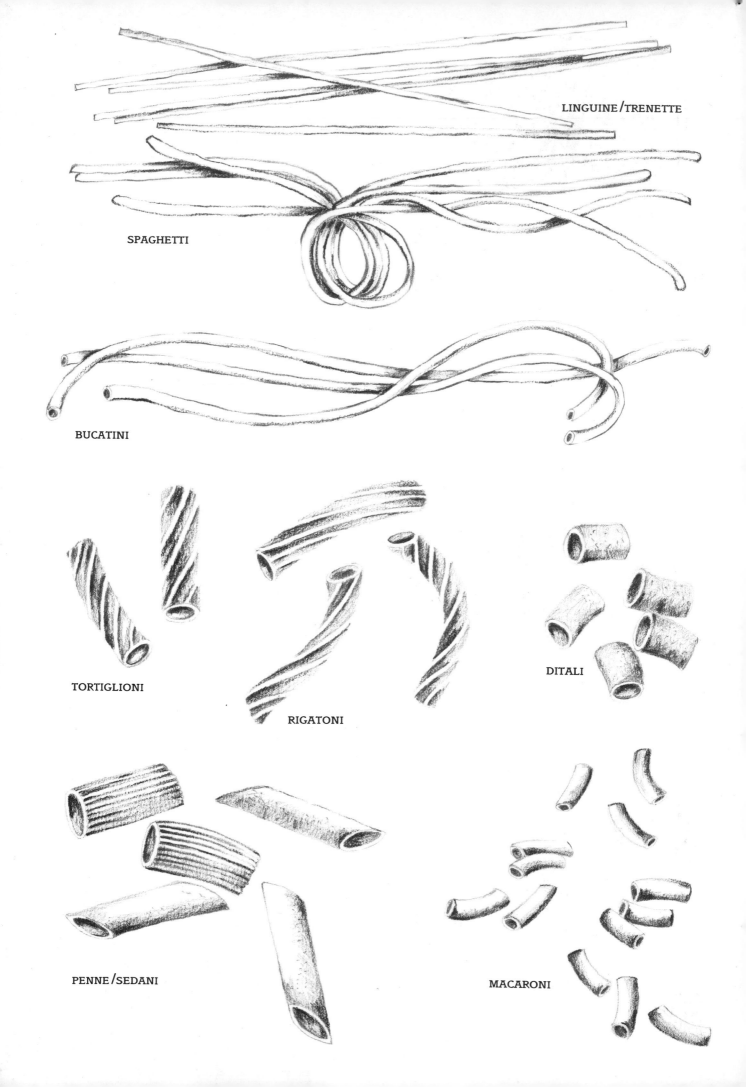

LINGUINE/TRENETTE

SPAGHETTI

BUCATINI

TORTIGLIONI

RIGATONI

DITALI

PENNE/SEDANI

MACARONI